cocktail

cocktail

OONA VAN DEN BERG

LORENZ BOOKS

Bracketed terms are intended for American readers.

For all recipes, **quantities** are given in both **metric** & **imperial** measures &, where appropriate, measures are also given in **standard cups** & **spoons**. Follow one set, but not a mixture, because they are **not interchangeable**. Standard **spoon** & **cup measures** are level. 1 tsp = 5 ml, 1 tbsp = 15 ml, 1 cup = 250 ml/8 fl oz

Australian standard **tablespoons** are 20 ml. Australian readers should use 3 tsp in place of 1 tbsp for measuring small quantities of sugar, liquids, etc.

Medium (US large) eggs are used unless otherwise stated.

Some of the recipes in this book previously appeared in **50 Classic Cocktails**

Many thanks to alcohol aficionados:
Michael Fussell, James Fischer, Nicky Moores, Adrian Heath-Saunders

This edition is published by Lorenz Books
Lorenz Books is an imprint of Anness Publishing Ltd
Hermes House, 88–89 Blackfriars Road, London SE1 8HA
tel. 020 7401 2077; fax 020 7633 9499
www.lorenzbooks.com; info@anness.com

© Anness Publishing Ltd 2001, 2003

UK agent: The Manning Partnership Ltd, tel. 01225 478444; fax 01225 478440; sales@manning-partnership.co.uk
UK distributor: Grantham Book Services Ltd, tel. 01476 541080; fax 01476 541061; orders@gbs.tbs-ltd.co.uk
North American agent/distributor: National Book Network, tel. 301 459 3366; fax 301 429 5746; www.nbnbooks.com
Australian agent/distributor: Pan Macmillan Australia, tel. 1300 135 113; fax 1300 135 103; customer.service@macmillan.com.au
New Zealand agent/distributor: David Bateman Ltd, tel. (09) 415 7664; fax (09) 415 8892

A CIP catalogue record for this book is available from the British Library.

Publisher Joanna Lorenz
Managing Editor Judith Simons
Editor Charlotte Berman
Photography Steve Baxter, Gus Filgate, William Lingwood, Simon Smith
Food for Photography Caroline Barty, Oona van den Berg, Joanna Farrow, Jane Stevenson, Carol Tennant
Design Norma Martin
Production Controller Joanna King

10 9 8 7 6 5 4 3 2 1

cocktail

introduction

Colourful, EXOTIC and **COOL** – COCKTAILS are the **most** STYLISH drinks of the 21st Century. Whether you want a **short**, sharp, **fizzy** shock with a twist of **lime**, something long and **smooth**, or a refreshing ICY cooler in a frosted glass, you can find them **all** in this **COSMOPOLITAN** collection of **chic** concoctions to soothe, excite, **INDULGE** and IMPRESS.

techniques, tips & garnishes

ATTENTION TO **DETAIL** IS THE DIFFERENCE BETWEEN A **GOOD** COCKTAIL AND A **FANTASTIC** COCKTAIL, SO LET YOUR **CREATIVE** JUICES FLOW AND DISCOVER HOW A **DELICATELY** DECORATED ICE CUBE, A CAREFULLY **FROSTED** GLASS OR AN **UNUSUAL** KUMQUAT **GARNISH** CAN TURN THE SIMPLEST OF **CONCOCTIONS** INTO A **WORK OF ART**.

crushing ice

Rather than simply using ice cubes to chill cocktails, some recipes, such as those for Dickson's Bloody Mary and Mint Julep, require cracked or crushed ice for adding to glasses, while others can benefit from a finely crushed ice snow for blending. These types of ice will melt faster than conventional ice cubes, so either serve the icy drinks the moment you've made them, or store them in the fridge until they are needed.

The easiest way to crush ice is to lay a cloth on a worksurface, cover half of the cloth with ice cubes and fold the cloth over (or if you have an ice cloth bag place the ice in that). Using the end of a rolling pin or a wooden mallet, strike the ice firmly, several times, until you achieve the required fineness. Spoon or scrape the crushed ice or ice snow into glasses or a jug. Fine ice snow must be used immediately, but cracked or roughly crushed ice can be stored in the freezer in plastic bags.

making decorative ice cubes

Adding decorative ice cubes to a cocktail is an easy and effective way to turn a simple cocktail into something much more exciting. As well as adding small colourful and fragrant leaves or fruit you can also flavour and colour ice cubes with fruit juices or angostura bitters and freeze as normal.

To make decorative ice cubes, half fill each compartment of an ice cube tray with water and place in the freezer for 2–3 hours or until the water has frozen. Prepare the decoration — berries, redcurrants, olives, mint leaves, lemon rind, raisins and borage flowers all work well — and dip each decoration briefly in water. Place one or two decorations in each ice cube compartment and freeze again. Top up the ice cube trays with water and return to the freezer to freeze completely. Use as required.

frosting glasses

Frosting adds both to the look and the taste of a cocktail. Celery salt, grated coconut, grated chocolate, coloured sugars and cocoa all work well, but make sure that you match the frosting with the taste of the cocktail. You can even frost glasses in advance and then place the glass in the frige to chill, until needed.

Take a clean, dry glass and hold it upside down. Rub the rim of the glass with the cut surface of a lemon, lime, orange or even a slice of fresh pineapple. Keeping the glass upside down, dip the rim into a shallow layer of salt, sugar or other ingredient. Re-dip the glass, if necessary, so the rim is well coated. Stand the glass upright and leave it until the salt, sugar or other ingredient has dried on the rim. Use at once or chill.

shaking cocktails

Cocktails that contain sugar syrups or creams, such as a Havana Cobbler or Grasshopper, require more than just a stir, while it is well known that the classic Vodka Martini can be shaken or stirred. By adding crushed or cracked ice to your cocktail shaker you can combine and chill the ingredients all at the same time. It goes without saying that fizzy cocktails should never be shaken! Remember that it is only possible to shake one or two servings at a time.

Fill the cocktail shaker two-thirds full with ice cubes and pour in the spirits. Add the mixers, if not sparkling, and the flavouring ingredients. Put the lid of the shaker on. Hold the shaker firmly, keeping the lid in place with one hand. Shake vigorously for about 10 seconds to blend simple concoctions and for 20–30 seconds for drinks with sugar syrups or eggs. By this time the outside of the shaker should feel chilled. Remove the small lid and pour into the prepared glass, using a strainer if the shaker is not already fitted with one.

making sugar syrups

Because it immediately blends with the other ingredients, basic sugar syrup is often preferable to crystal sugars for sweetening cocktails. Sugar syrups can be flavoured with almost any ingredient, although raspberries, black or redcurrants, plums and peaches probably make the most delicious syrups of all.

To make 750ml/1¼ pints/3 cups of basic sugar syrup place 350g/12oz of caster (superfine) sugar in a heavy pan with 600ml/1 pint/2½ cups water and heat gently over a low heat. Stir with a wooden spoon until the sugar has dissolved. Brush the sides of the pan with a pastry brush dampened in water to remove any sugar crystals that might cause the sugar syrup to crystallize. Bring to the boil for 3–5 minutes. Skim off any scum and, when no more appears, remove the pan from the heat. When cool, pour into clean, dry, airtight bottles. Keep chilled for one month.

For flavoured syrups, wash and crush 900g/2lb very ripe soft or stoned (pitted) fruit using a rolling pin, wooden pestle or a potato masher. Cover and leave overnight. Strain the purée through a cloth bag or piece of muslin (cheesecloth). Gather the corners of the cloth together and twist them tightly to remove as much juice as possible. Measure the amount of juice and add 225g/8oz sugar to every 300ml/½ pint/1¼ cups fruit juice. Place the pan over a low heat and gently stir until all the sugar has dissolved. Continue as in the recipe for basic sugar syrup above. The syrup will keep in the refrigerator for up to one month.

steeping spirits (liquors)

Steeping any spirit (liquor) with a strong flavouring ingredient, such as chillies, creates an interestingly flavoured spirit. Other great combinations include gin with cumin seeds, star anise or juniper berries; brandy with peeled and sliced root ginger or cloves; vodka with raisins or black peppercorns and rum with vanilla pods (beans). The amounts used depend on personal taste.

To make 1 litre/1¾ pints/4 cups chilli vodka or sherry, wash and dry 25–50g/1–2oz small red chillies, discarding any that are less than perfect. Using a cocktail stick, prick the chillies all over to release their flavours. Pack the chillies tightly into a sterilized bottle and top up with vodka or sherry. Fit the cork tightly and leave in a dark place for at least ten days or up to two months.

garnishes

It is far more eye-catching not to overdress cocktails, otherwise they all too quickly look like a fruit salad. Less is best! Edible garnishes are always best and they should reflect the contents of the glass.

Frosting glasses with salt or sugar is a simple but effective touch. Citrus fruits are widely used because they stay appetizing to look at and can be cut in advance and kept covered in the refrigerator, for a day, until required. Apple, pear and banana are also suitable, but dip them in lemon juice first to prevent them from discolouring when exposed to the air.

Soft fruit, such as strawberries, fresh cherries, peaches, apricots, redcurrants and blackberries make fabulous splashes of colour and add a delicious flavour. Take advantage of them when they are in season, as otherwise their price may be restrictive.

Maraschino cherries are a popular option and the never-ending supply of exotic fruits available all year round, such as mango, pineapple, kumquat, physalis, lychee and star fruit, offers endless decorative possibilities.

Not all garnishes and decorations are fruit based. Grated chocolate, sticks of cinnamon and nutmeg adorn eggnogs and eggflips, while some Martinis call for a green olive – always opt for those in brine and not in oil. Plain or steeped-chilli vodka can stand pickled chillies and the Gibson (a dry Martini cocktail) wouldn't be a Gibson without a white pearl onion to complete it.

fizzy

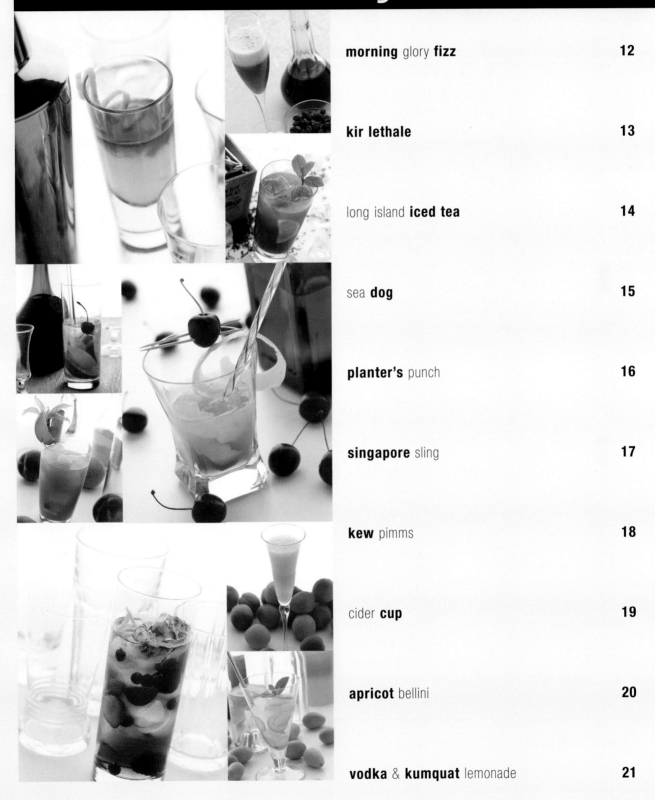

ingredients

⅔ measure/15ml/1 tbsp **brandy**

¼ measure/5ml/1 tsp
orange curaçao

¼ measure/5ml/1 tsp
lemon juice

dash **anisette**

2 dashes **angostura bitters**

soda water, to taste

twist of **lemon rind**, to decorate

morning glory fizz

A GOOD **EARLY MORNING** DRINK, WHICH SHOULD BE CONSUMED AS SOON AS IT IS MADE, BEFORE IT LOSES ITS **FLAVOUR** AND **FIZZINESS**.

variation

Shake together an egg white, sugar syrup to taste, the juice of ½ lemon and ½ lime and gin or whisky instead of the brandy and add a splash of Chartreuse. Shake well and top up with soda.

method

SERVES 1

1 Pour the brandy, curaçao, lemon juice and anisette into a cocktail shaker containing ice and shake for 20 seconds.

2 Strain the drink into a small chilled cocktail glass.

3 Add the angostura bitters to taste and top up with soda water.

4 Using a canelle knife cut a long thin piece of lemon rind. Curl the lemon rind into a tight coil and add to the drink.

kir lethale

method

SERVES 6

1 Place a vodka-soaked raisin at the bottom of each glass.

2 Add a teaspoon of vodka or the vodka from the steeped raisins, if using, to each glass.

3 Divide the crème de cassis equally between the glasses.

4 Only when ready to serve, top up each glass with the champagne or dry sparkling wine.

TO MAKE THE **RAISINS** FOR THIS COCKTAIL REALLY PLUMP AND JUICY, **SOAK** THEM FOR A FEW HOURS, OR OVERNIGHT, IN A GLASS FULL OF **VODKA**.

variation
For Kir Framboise, use crème de framboise or raspberry syrup and raspberry-flavoured vodka.

ingredients

6 **vodka-soaked raisins**

1⅓ measure/30ml/2 tbsp
vodka or **raisin vodka**

3 measures/70ml/4½ tbsp
crème de cassis

1 bottle brut **champagne** or dry sparkling wine, chilled

ingredients

½ measure/10ml/2 tsp
white rum
½ measure/10ml/2 tsp **vodka**
½ measure/10ml/2 tsp **gin**
½ measure/10ml/2 tsp **Grand**
Marnier or Cointreau
1 measure/25ml/1½ tbsp cold
Earl Grey tea
juice ½ **lemon**
cola, chilled, to taste
slices of **lemon** and a large sprig
of **mint**, to decorate

long island iced tea

A **LONG, POTENT** DRINK THAT HAS AN
INTOXICATING EFFECT, WHICH IS WELL
DISGUISED BY THE **COLA**. FOR A SIMPLER
VERSION, USE **EQUAL** QUANTITIES OF **RUM,**
COINTREAU, TEQUILA AND **LEMON JUICE**
AND **TOP UP** WITH **COLA**.

method

SERVES 4-6

1 Fill a bar glass with cracked ice and add the rum, vodka, gin and
Grand Marnier or Cointreau.

2 Add the cold Earl Grey tea to the spirits in the bar glass.

3 Stir well for 30 seconds to chill the spirits and the tea.

4 Add the lemon juice, to taste.

5 Strain into a highball tumbler filled with ice cubes and lemon slices.

6 Add the chilled cola, according to taste, and add a sprig of fresh mint.

sea dog

A LONG **WHISKY** DRINK WITH A **CITRUS TWIST**. FOR A **SWEETER DRINK**, ADD A SECOND **SUGAR LUMP**; IF INCLUDING **DRAMBUIE**, ONLY USE ONE.

method

SERVES 1

1 Put the sugar cube at the bottom of a Collins glass, add the bitters and allow to soak into the sugar cube.

2 Add the orange and lemon wedges and, using a muddler, press the juices from the fruit.

3 Fill the glass with cracked ice.

4 Add the whisky or Drambuie and the Benedictine and mix together well with a swizzle stick for 20 seconds.

5 Top up with chilled soda water.

6 Serve with the muddler, so that more juice can be pressed from the fruit according to personal taste; decorate with a maraschino cherry.

ingredients

1–2 **sugar cubes**
2 dashes **angostura bitters**
2 **orange wedges**
2 **lemon wedges**
⅔ measure/15ml/1 tbsp **whisky**
    or **Drambuie**
1 measure/25ml/1½ tbsp
    Benedictine
2 measures/45ml/3 tbsp **soda water**, chilled
maraschino cherry, to decorate

variation
Use gin in place of the whisky and Pimms in place of the Benedictine.

ingredients

1 measure/25ml/1½ tbsp
lime juice
1 measure/25ml/1½ tbsp
orange juice (optional)
2 measures/45ml/3 tbsp
dark rum
½ measure/10ml/2 tsp
grenadine
dash **angostura bitters**
soda water or
lemonade, chilled
peach slices and a **physalis**,
to decorate

planter's punch

THIS LONG REFRESHING **OLD COLONIAL DRINK** ORIGINATES FROM THE SUGAR PLANTATIONS FOUND THROUGHOUT THE **WEST INDIES**.

variation
Add 1 measure/25ml/1   tbsp cold Assam tea, for a different tang.

method

SERVES 1

1 Squeeze the lime and orange juices and add to a glass filled with ice.

2 Add the dark rum and the grenadine and mix together for about 20 seconds.

3 Add a dash of bitters to the bottom of a tumbler of decorative ice cubes.

4 Strain the rum and grenadine mixture into the chilled tumbler.

5 Top up with plenty of chilled soda water or lemonade.

6 Decorate with peach slices and a physalis.

singapore sling

method

THE ORIGINS OF THIS **CLASSIC THIRST QUENCHER** LIE FAR AWAY TO THE EAST.

1 Pour the gin into a bar glass of ice and mix with the lemon juice and sugar.

2 Strain the cocktail into a tumbler full of cracked ice.

variation

Substitute Benedictine for the Cointreau for a Straits Sling, and add ginger beer instead of soda water for a Raffles Bar Sling.

3 Top up the cocktail with chilled soda water, to taste.

4 Add the Cointreau and the cherry brandy, but do not stir.

5 To decorate, use a vegetable peeler or sharp knife to cut a long piece of rind round and round the lemon.

6 Arrange the lemon rind in the glass. Thread the cherry on to two cocktail sticks and add to the rim of the glass.

ingredients

2 measures/45ml/3 tbsp gin

juice 1 **lemon**

5ml/1 tsp **caster (superfine) sugar**

soda water, chilled

⅔ measure/15ml/1 tbsp **Cointreau**

⅔ measure/15ml/1 tbsp **cherry brandy**

1 **lemon**, to decorate

black cherry, to decorate

ingredients

1 measure/25ml/1½ tbsp
sweet vermouth

1 measure/25ml/1½ tbsp
orange curaçao

⅔ measure/15ml/1tbsp **vodka**

⅔ measure/15ml/1tbsp **gin**

⅔ measure/15ml/1 tbsp
cherry brandy

assorted soft **summer fruits**

1–2 dashes **angostura bitters**

2 measures/45ml/3 tbsp
American dry
ginger ale, chilled

2 measures/45ml/3 tbsp
lemonade, chilled

1 **lemon**, to decorate

lemon balm or **mint leaves**,
to decorate

kew pimms

A **DELICIOUS** CONCOCTION THAT INCLUDES
VERMOUTH, CURAÇAO, AND CHERRY
BRANDY, SERVED OVER **SUMMER FRUIT**.

method

SERVES 1

1 Measure the vermouth, curaçao, vodka, gin and cherry brandy into a
bar glass filled with ice and stir well to chill.

2 Strain into a tall highball tumbler full of ice cubes and assorted soft
summer fruits.

3 Add the bitters and then pour in equal quantities of chilled ginger ale
and lemonade to taste.

4 To make the lemon triangles, pare a thin piece of lemon rind from the
lemon. Cut the rind into a rectangle and cut a slit three-quarters of the
way across the lemon rind. Turn the rectangle and repeat from the
other side. Twist to form a triangle, crossing the ends to secure.

5 Add the lemon triangle to the drink with lemon balm or mint leaves.

variation
Top up the spirit base with champagne, sparkling wine or tonic water.

cider cup

CUPS MAKE AN **EXCELLENT** LONG AND **REFRESHING** DRINK FOR AN APERITIF OR **PARTY**. MIX UP JUST BEFORE SERVING.

method

SERVES 6

1 Partly fill a pitcher with cracked ice and add the lemon rind and slices of orange.

2 Add the sherry, brandy, curaçao and amaretto to the ice and stir well to mix.

3 Pour in the cider and stir gently with a long swizzle stick.

4 Using a canelle knife, peel the cucumber around in a continuous piece, to produce a spiral. Serve the cocktail in chilled glasses, decorated with the fruit and a twist of cucumber peel.

ingredients

rind of 1 **lemon**

slices of **orange**

5 measures/120ml/4fl oz/½ cup **pale sherry**

3 measures/70ml/4½ tbsp **brandy or clove brandy**

3 measures/70 ml/4½ tbsp **white curaçao**

2 measures/45 ml/3 tbsp **amaretto**

600ml/1 pint/2½ cups good quality **medium sweet (hard) cider**

cucumber, to decorate

variation
Instead of brandy, use Calvados for a richer flavour and add a little maraschino cherry juice to give more colour.

ingredients

3 **apricots**

½ measure/10ml/2 tsp **lemon juice**

½ measure/10ml/2 tsp **sugar syrup**

2 measures/45ml/3 tbsp **apricot brandy** or **peach schnapps**

1 bottle **brut champagne** or **dry sparkling wine**, chilled

variation

Instead of apricots and apricot brandy, use fresh raspberries and raspberry-infused gin or syrup.

apricot bellini

THIS IS A VERSION OF THE FAMOUS **APÉRITIF** SERVED AT **HARRY'S BAR** IN **VENICE**. INSTEAD OF THE USUAL **PEACHES** AND PEACH **BRANDY**, APRICOT **NECTAR** AND APRICOT BRANDY MAKE THIS A TEMPTING VARIATION.

method

SERVES 6-8

1 Plunge the apricots into boiling water for 2 minutes, or until the skins have loosened.

2 Peel off the skins of the apricots, remove the stones and discard both.

3 Process the apricot flesh with the lemon juice until you have a smooth purée. Sweeten to taste with sugar syrup, then sieve.

4 Add the brandy or peach schnapps to the apricot nectar and mix together to combine.

5 Divide the apricot nectar between the chilled champagne flutes.

6 Top up the glasses with chilled champagne or sparkling wine.

vodka & kumquat lemonade

A **MILD-SOUNDING** NAME FOR A **STRONG** CONCOCTION OF **KUMQUAT** AND **PEPPERCORN**-FLAVOURED **VODKA** AND WHITE **CURAÇAO**.

method

SERVES 2

1 Slice the kumquats thickly and add to the vodka in an airtight jar with the cracked black peppercorns, if using. Leave aside for a couple of hours, overnight or up to a month.

2 Fill a jug with cracked ice and then add the curaçao or orange syrup, the lemon juice and the kumquat-flavoured vodka with the sliced kumquats.

3 Using a long swizzle stick, mix together well.

4 Add the mineral or soda water and a few fresh mint leaves and gently stir everything together.

5 Pour the drink (lemonade) into chilled glasses of ice.

6 Add slices of vodka-soaked kumquats to the glasses and decorate with more mint sprigs

> ### variation
> Use elderflower or fruit cordial, with gin or vodka as the base, and top up with soda or tonic water.

ingredients

75g/3oz **kumquats**

5 measures/120ml/4fl oz/ ½ cup **vodka**

3 **black peppercorns**, cracked (optional)

⅔ measure/15ml/1 tbsp **white curaçao** or **orange syrup**

⅔ measure/15ml/1 tbsp **lemon juice**

7 measures/150ml/¼ pint/ ⅔ cup **mineral** or **soda water**

sprigs of **mint**, to decorate

creamy

ingredients

1 measure/25ml/1½ tbsp **brandy**

1 measure/25ml/1½ tbsp
crème de cacao

1 measure/25ml/1½ tbsp
double (heavy) cream

whole **nutmeg**, grated,
to decorate

brandy alexander

method

SERVES 1

A **WARMING DIGESTIF**, MADE FROM A
BLEND OF CRÈME DE CACAO, BRANDY AND
CREAM, THAT CAN BE SERVED AT THE END
OF THE MEAL WITH **COFFEE**.

1 Half fill the cocktail shaker with ice and pour in the brandy, crème de
cacao and, finally, the cream.

2 Shake for about 20 seconds, to mix together well.

variation

Warm the brandy and the double cream gently and add to a blender with the
crème de cacao. Whizz until frothy. Serve with a cinnamon stick.

3 Strain the chilled cocktail into a small wine glass.

4 Finely grate a little nutmeg over the top of the cocktail.

b52

THIS **COCKTAIL** DEPENDS ON THE DIFFERENCE IN **SPECIFIC** WEIGHT OR **DENSITY** OF EACH OF THE **LIQUEURS** TO REMAIN STRICTLY **SEPARATED** IN LAYERS.

method

SERVES 1

1 In a small shooter or pousse-café glass, pour a 2cm/¾ in layer of Kahlúa.

2 Hold a cold teaspoon upside-down, only just touching the surface of the Kahlúa and the side of the glass,

3 Slowly and carefully pour the Grand Marnier over the back of the teaspoon, to create a second layer.

4 In the same way, carefully pour the Bailey's over the back of a second clean teaspoon, to create a final layer. This layer in fact will form the middle layer and push the Grand Marnier to the top!

ingredients

1 measure/25 ml/1½ tbsp
Kahlúa
1 measure/25 ml/1½ tbsp
Grand Marnier
1 measure/25 ml/1½ tbsp
Bailey's Irish Cream

---

variation

Create a similar layered effect with equal quantities of Bailey's, Kahlúa and vodka, layered in that order. Or try Chartreuse, cherry brandy and kümmel, with cumin seeds floated on the top.

ingredients

2 measures/45ml/3 tbsp
crème de menthe

2 measures/45ml/3 tbsp light
crème de cacao

2 measures/45ml/3 tbsp
double (heavy) cream

melted **plain (semisweet)**
chocolate, to decorate

grasshopper

A MINTED, **CREAMY** COCKTAIL IN AN
ATTRACTIVE SHADE OF **GREEN**. IF YOU USE
DARK **CRÈME DE CACAO** THE COCKTAIL
WILL NOT BE AS **VIBRANT** A GREEN COLOUR
BUT YOU'LL FIND THAT IT WILL **TASTE** JUST
AS GOOD.

method   SERVES 1

1 Measure the crème de menthe and crème de cacao into a cocktail
shaker and add the cream.

2 Add some cracked ice and shake well for 20 seconds.

3 Strain the cocktail into a tumbler of finely-cracked ice.

4 To decorate, spread the melted chocolate evenly over a plastic board
and leave to cool and harden. Using a sharp knife draw the blade
across the chocolate to create curls. Add to the top of the cocktail
and serve.

variation
Process in a blender, with crushed ice, for a smoother consistency. For a
Scandinavian Freeze, mix vodka with crème de cacao and a scoop of vanilla ice
cream and process until just smooth.

blue hawaiian

THIS DRINK CAN BE DECORATED AS FLAMBOYANTLY AS **CARMEN MIRANDA'S** HEADDRESS WITH A MIXTURE OF **FRUITS** AND **LEAVES**. AN **EYE-CATCHING** COLOUR, BUT YOU'LL FIND IT VERY DRINKABLE.

method

SERVES 1

1 Put the curaçao, coconut cream and white rum in a blender. Process very briefly until the colour is even.

2 Place ice cubes between a dishtowel and crush to a fine snow with a wooden hammer or rolling pin.

3 Add the pineapple juice to the blender and process the mixture once more, until frothy.

4 Spoon the crushed ice into a large cocktail glass or goblet.

5 Pour the cocktail from the blender over the crushed ice.

6 Decorate with the pineapple leaves and wedge, a prickly pear slice, a lime wedge and a maraschino cherry. Serve with a drinking straws.

> ### variation
> Pour equal quantities of vodka and blue curaçao over ice. Top up with lemonade for a Blue Lagoon or add equal quantities of gin and curaçao, plus angostura bitters, for a Blue Cloak.

ingredients

1 measure/25ml/1½ tbsp
blue curaçao
1 measure/25ml/½ tbsp
coconut cream
2 measures/45ml/3 tbsp
white rum
2 measures/45ml/3 tbsp
pineapple juice

To decorate
leaves and wedge of **pineapple**
slice of **prickly pear**
wedge of **lime**
maraschino cherry

ingredients

2 measures/45ml/3 tbsp
Galliano

1 measure/25ml/1½ tbsp
orange juice, chilled

1 measure/25ml/1½ tbsp
pineapple juice, chilled

1 measure/25ml/1½ tbsp **white**
or **orange curaçao**

1 measure/25ml/1½ tbsp
coconut cream

30ml/2 tbsp **pineapple juice**,
to decorate

25g/1oz **caster (superfine)**
sugar, to decorate

golden start

A **DELICIOUS** MIX OF GALLIANO, **ORANGE**,
PINEAPPLE AND **COCONUT** CREAM.

method

SERVES 1

1 Put the Galliano, orange and pineapple juices, and curaçao in a
blender and process together.

2 Add the coconut cream with a tablespoon of fine ice snow and
process until smooth and frothy.

3 Rub the rim of the shorts tumbler with pineapple juice and invert the
glass into a saucer of sugar, to frost the rim.

4 Pour the cocktail into the prepared glass while still frothy.

> **variation**
> Substitute light crème de cacao for the curaçao, to give that
> extra tropical twist.

african coffee

IN PARTS OF **AFRICA**, COFFEE IS OFTEN DRUNK WITH **CONDENSED MILK**. THIS RECIPE IS AN ADAPTATION OF AN AFRICAN BREW WITH A **LUXURIOUS** LIQUEUR FINISH.

method

SERVES 1

1 Add the coffee, condensed milk and liqueur to a shaker and mix well.

2 Serve over ice-cubes in tall glasses.

---
variation
Other chocolate- and coconut-based liqueurs, such as Malibu, work equally well in this recipe.
---

ingredients

250ml/8fl oz/1 cup
cold strong coffee
scant 2 measures/40ml/8 tsp
condensed milk
scant 1 measure/20ml/4 tsp
crème de cacao
ice cubes, to serve, optional

---
tip
To make strong coffee use 70g/3 oz **coffee** per 1 litre/ 1¾ pints/4 cups of **water**, or in this case add 17g/½ oz of **coffee** to 250ml/8fl oz/1 cup of **water**.

ingredients

1 litre/1¾ pints/4 cups **milk**

350g/12oz/1½ cups **sugar**

2.5ml/½ tsp **bicarbonate of soda**

1 **cinnamon stick**, about 15cm/6in long

12 large **egg yolks**

300ml/½ pint/1¼ cups **dark rum**

rompope

LEGEND HAS IT THAT THIS **RICH EGGNOG** WAS FIRST MADE IN THE **KITCHENS** OF A **CONVENT** IN **MEXICO**. SOME VERSIONS ARE THICKENED WITH **GROUND ALMONDS** OR SERVED WITH **FRESH SOFT** FRUITS SUCH AS RASPBERRIES. IT IS **TRADITIONAL** TO **SEAL** BOTTLES OF ROMPOPE WITH **ROLLED CORN HUSKS** OR CORN COBS WHICH HAVE BEEN STRIPPED OF THEIR CORN.

method

SERVES 6

1 Pour the milk into a saucepan and stir in the sugar and bicarbonate of soda. Add the cinnamon stick.

2 Place the pan over a moderate heat and bring the mixture to the boil, stirring constantly. Immediately pour the mixture into a bowl and cool to room temperature. Remove the cinnamon stick, squeezing it gently to release any liquid.

3 Put the egg yolks in a heatproof bowl over a pan of simmering water and whisk until the mixture is very thick and pale.

4 Add the whisked yolks to the milk mixture a little at a time, beating after each addition.

5 Return the mixture to a clean pan, place over a low heat and cook until the mixture thickens and the back of the spoon is visible when a finger is drawn along it.

6 Stir in the rum, pour into sterilized bottles and seal tightly with stoppers or clear film. Chill until required. Serve rompope very cold. It will keep for up to 1 week in the fridge.

ingredients

5 measures/120ml/4fl oz/½ cup
port

2 measures/45ml/3 tbsp
curaçao

scant 1 measure 20ml/4 tsp
very strong **coffee**

½ measure/10ml/2 tsp **icing
(confectioner's) sugar**

2 **eggs**

scant 1 measure 20ml/4 tsp
condensed milk

2⅔ measures 60ml/4 tbsp
crushed **ice**

variation

Most orange-based liqueurs, such as
Grand Marnier, Cointreau, Orange
Nassau and triple sec, could be used
in place of the curaçao, if
not available.

lisbon flip

THE COFFEE IN THIS RECIPE PROVIDES A
FLAVOURFUL UNDERTONE IN AN
INTERESTING AND **SATISFYING** COCKTAIL.

method

SERVES 6–8

1 Place all the ingredients in a cocktail shaker.

2 Shake vigorously and serve immediately in cocktail glasses. Top with
the finely grated chocolate and orange rind.

ingredients

1 **banana**, peeled and sliced

1 thick slice **pineapple**, peeled

3 measures/70ml/4½ tbsp
   pineapple juice

1 scoop **strawberry ice cream**
   or **sorbet**

1 measure/25ml/1½ tbsp
   coconut milk

   1⅓ measure/30ml/2 tbsp
   grenadine

wedges of **pineapple** and
   stemmed **maraschino**
   cherries, to decorate

blushing piña colada

THIS IS **GOOD** WITH OR WITHOUT THE **RUM**.
DON'T BE **TEMPTED** TO PUT ROUGHLY
CRUSHED ICE INTO THE **BLENDER**; IT WILL
NOT BE AS SMOOTH AND WILL **RUIN** THE
BLADES. MAKE SURE YOU **CRUSH IT**
WELL FIRST.

method

SERVES 2

1 Roughly chop the banana. Cut two small wedges from the pineapple
for decoration and reserve. Cut up the remainder of the pineapple and
add to the blender with the banana.

2 Add the pineapple juice to the blender and process until the mixture is
a smooth purée.

3 Add the strawberry ice cream or sorbet with the coconut milk and a
small scoop of finely crushed ice, and process until smooth.

4 Pour into two large, well-chilled cocktail glasses.

5 Pour the grenadine syrup slowly on top of the Piña Colada; it will filter
through the drink in a dappled effect.

6 Decorate each glass with a wedge of pineapple and a stemmed cherry
and serve with drinking straws.

variation

For classic Piña Colada use vanilla ice cream and 1 measure white rum. For a
Passionate Encounter, blend 2 scoops passion fruit sorbet and ⅔
measure/15ml/1 tbsp coconut milk with a measure each of pineapple and
apricot juice.

coffee &
chocolate flip

DRAMBUIE CAN BE USED INSTEAD OF **BRANDY** FOR A HINT OF **HONEY**, BUT DON'T ADD THE SUGAR. SUBSTITUTE TIA MARIA FOR THE **KAHLÚA**, FOR A **LESS SWEET** VERSION.

method
SERVES 1

1 Separate the egg and lightly beat the egg white until frothy and white.

2 In a separate bowl or glass, beat the egg yolk with the sugar.

3 In a small pan, gently warm together the brandy, Kahlúa, coffee granules and cream.

4 Whisk the cooled cream mixture into the egg yolk.

5 Add the egg white to the egg and cream and pour the mixture briefly back and forth between two glasses, until the mixture is smooth.

6 Pour into a tall glass over coarsely crushed ice and sprinkle the top with drinking chocolate powder.

---

variation
Shake together equal quantities of Kahlúa, chocolate-flavoured milk and coffee. Serve on the rocks.

---

ingredients

1 **egg**
5ml/1 tsp **caster (superfine) sugar**
1 measure/25ml/1½ tbsp **brandy**
1 measure/25ml/½ tbsp **Kahlúa**
¼ measure/5ml/1 tsp **instant coffee** granules
3 measures/70ml/4½ tbsp **double (heavy) cream**
drinking chocolate powder or **grated chocolate**, to decorate

fruity

ingredients

5 measures/120ml/4fl oz/½ cup
prune juice

2 measures/45ml/3 tbsp
Amaretto

1 measure/25ml/1½ tbsp
Cointreau

hooded claw

SYRUPY SWEET PRUNE JUICE WITH
AMARETTO AND **COINTREAU** MAKES A
DELICIOUS DIGESTIF WHEN POURED OVER
FINELY CRUSHED ICE **SNOW**.

variation

Mix 6 parts prune juice with 1 part elderflower cordial, for a tangy, non-alcoholic
version. Serve it on the rocks and super-cold.

method

SERVES 4–6

1 Pour the prune juice, Amaretto and Cointreau together into a cocktail
shaker half filled with ice.

2 Shake the cocktail for 20 seconds, to chill well.

3 Loosely fill four small liqueur glasses with finely crushed ice snow.

4 Strain the drink into the glasses and serve with short drinking straws.

gin crusta

PREPARE THE GLASS **IN ADVANCE** AND KEEP IT **CHILLED** IN THE **FRIDGE** READY FOR **INSTANT USE!** THE DEPTH OF **PINK** COLOUR WILL DEPEND ON THE STRENGTH OF THE **MARASCHINO** CHERRY JUICE.

method

SERVES 1

1 Cut both ends off the lemon and, using a sharp knife or canelle knife, peel the lemon thinly, as you would an apple, in one long continuous piece.

ingredients

1 **lemon**
1⅓ measure/30ml/2 tbsp **golden granulated sugar**
3 dashes **sugar syrup**
2 dashes **maraschino cherry juice**
2 dashes **angostura bitters**
1 measure/25 ml/1½ tbsp dry **gin**

---

variation
Make in the same way with whisky, Southern Comfort, brandy or rum.

---

2 Halve the whole lemon and rub the edge of a glass with one half.

3 Turn the glass upside-down and dip it into the granulated sugar, to create a decorative rim,

4 Arrange the lemon rind in a scroll on the inside of the glass.

5 Place the sugar syrup, maraschino cherry juice, angostura bitters, gin and juice of 1/4 of the lemon in a cocktail shaker, half filled with ice.

6 Shake for about 30 seconds and carefully strain into the prepared glass,

ingredients

2 measures/45ml/3 tbsp
cranberry juice
1 measure/25ml/1½ tbsp **brandy**
2 measures/45ml/3 tbsp **pink**
grapefruit juice
2 measures/45ml/3 tbsp
Marsala

to decorate
redcurrant string,
1 **egg white**, lightly beaten,
15g/½oz **caster**
(superfine) sugar

cranberry kiss

A **DELICIOUS** FULL-FLAVOURED COCKTAIL,
WITH THE **TANG** OF CRANBERRY AND PINK
GRAPEFRUIT JUICES AND THE **SWEETNESS**
OF MARSALA.

method
SERVES 1

1 For the decoration, lightly brush the redcurrants with the egg white.

2 Shake caster sugar over the redcurrants, to cover them in a light frosting. Leave aside to dry.

3 Place the cranberry juice with the brandy and grapefruit juice in a cocktail shaker full of crushed ice and shake for 20 seconds to mix.

4 Strain into a well-chilled glass.

5 Tilt the glass slightly, before slowly pouring the Marsala into the drink down the side of the glass.

6 Serve decorated with the frosted redcurrant string.

variation
Shake together cranberry and pineapple juice with coconut milk. Add vodka or gin to taste.

tequila sunset

A VARIATION ON THE **POPULAR PARTY DRINK** WHICH CAN BE **MIXED** AND CHILLED IN A **JUG**, READY TO POUR INTO **GLASSES**, AND **FINISHED** OFF AT THE LAST MINUTE WITH THE ADDITION OF **CRÈME DE CASSIS** AND **HONEY**.

method

SERVES 1

1 Pour the tequila and then the lemon and orange juices straight into a well-chilled cocktail glass.

2 Using a swizzle stick, mix the ingredients by twisting the stick between the palms of your hands.

3 Drizzle the honey into the centre of the cocktail so that it falls and creates a layer at the bottom of the glass.

4 Add the crème de cassis, but do not stir. It will create a glowing layer above the honey at the bottom of the glass.

ingredients

1 measure/25ml/1½ tbsp **clear or golden tequila**

5 measures/120ml/4fl oz/½ cup **lemon juice**, chilled

1 measure/25ml/1½ tbsp **orange juice**, chilled

10–30ml/2tsp–2 tbsp **clear honey**

⅔ measure/15ml/1tbsp **crème de cassis**

variation
To make a Tequila Sunrise, mix 2 parts tequila with 6 parts orange.

ingredients

2 measures/45ml/3 tbsp **vodka**
or **chilli-flavoured vodka**
1 measure/25ml/½ tbsp
fino sherry
7 measures/150ml/¼ pint/
⅔ cup/5fl oz **tomato juice**
1 measure/25ml/1½ tbsp
lemon juice
10–15ml/2–3 tsp
Worcestershire sauce
2–3 dashes **Tabasco sauce**
2.5ml/½ tsp **creamed**
horseradish relish
5ml/1 tsp **celery salt**
salt and **ground black pepper**
celery stick, **stuffed green**
olives, **cherry tomato**,
to decorate

THIS RECIPE HAS PLENTY OF **CHARACTER,**
WITH THE **HORSERADISH,** SHERRY
AND **TABASCO**.

method   SERVES 1

1 Fill a bar glass or jug with cracked ice and add the vodka, sherry and
tomato juice. Stir well.

2 Add the lemon juice, Worcestershire and Tabasco sauces and the
horseradish, according to taste.

3 Add the celery salt, salt and pepper and stir until the glass has frosted
and the Bloody Mary is chilled.

4 Strain into a long tumbler, half filled with ice cubes,

5 Add a decorative stick of celery as a swizzle stick.

6 Finish off the cocktail by threading a cocktail stick with olives and a
cherry tomato, and add to the rim of the glass

variation
Use tequila in the place of the vodka for a Bloody Maria and use a clam juice
and tomato juice mixture for a Bloody Muddle.

apple sour

method

SERVES 1

FOR THOSE WITH **CONCERNS** ABOUT **EATING RAW EGG**, THIS VARIATION ON A BRANDY SOUR CAN BE MADE **WITHOUT** THE EGG WHITE. APPLEJACK OR **APPLE SCHNAPPS** ALSO WORKS WELL IN THIS RECIPE, IN PLACE OF THE **CALVADOS**.

1 Put the Calvados, lemon juice and caster sugar into a shaker of ice, with the angostura bitters and egg white, if using.

2 Shake together for 30 seconds.

3 Strain the cocktail into a tumbler of cracked ice.

4 Dip the red and green apple slices in lemon juice. Decorate the cocktail with the apple slices threaded on to a bamboo skewer.

ingredients

1 measure/25ml/1½ tbsp
Calvados
⅔ measure/15ml/1 tbsp
lemon juice
5ml/1 tsp **caster**
(superfine) sugar
dash **angostura bitters**
1 **egg white** (optional)
red and green apple slices
and **lemon juice**, to decorate

variation

Sours can also be made with Amaretto or tequila; add a splash of raspberry syrup or port to the glass just before serving.

harvey wallbanger

THE **NEXT STEP ON** FROM A SCREWDRIVER
– ADD A DASH OF **GALLIANO**. THOSE WHO
LIKE A **STRONGER** VERSION SHOULD ADD AN
EXTRA MEASURE OF **VODKA**.

method   SERVES 1

1 Pour the vodka, Galliano and orange juice into a bar glass of ice.

ingredients

1 measure/25ml/½ tbsp **vodka**
⅔ measure/15ml/1 tbsp **Galliano**
7 measures/150ml/¼ pint/
⅔ cup **orange juice**
½ small **orange**, to decorate

---

variation
Mix together the orange juice and
vodka with a splash of ginger wine,
pour into a glass and slowly pour the
Galliano on top.

---

2 Mix the cocktail and ice for 30 seconds, to chill it well.

3 Using a canelle knife, take a series of strips of rind off the orange, running from the top to the bottom of the fruit.

4 Use a small sharp knife to cut the orange evenly and thinly into slices.

5 Cut the orange slices in half and wedge them between cracked ice in a highball glass.

6 Strain the chilled cocktail into the prepared glass.

strawberry & banana preparado

SIMILAR TO A SMOOTHIE, THIS IS A **THICK, FRUITY, CREAMY** DRINK. LEAVE OUT THE ALCOHOL IF DESIRED.

ingredients

200g/7oz/2 cups **strawberries**, plus extra to decorate

2 **bananas**

115g/4oz **block of creamed coconut**

120ml/4fl oz/½ cup **water**

175ml/6fl oz/¾ cup **white rum**

60ml/4 tbsp **grenadine**

method

SERVES 4

1 Hull the strawberries and chop them in halves or quarters if they are large fruits. Peel the bananas and chop them into rough chunks.

2 Put the fruit in a food processor or blender, crumble in the coconut and add the water. Process until smooth, scraping down the sides of the goblet as necessary.

3 Add the rum, grenadine, and ten ice cubes, crushing the ice first unless you have a heavy-duty processor. Blend until smooth and thick. Serve immediately, decorated with the extra strawberries.

ingredients

400g/14oz can/1⅔ cups **lychees**

2 **peaches**, sliced

600ml/1 pint/2½ cups **gin**

**For each person you
    will need**

1 measure/25ml/
    1½ tbsp **Pimms**

2–3 dashes **angostura bitters**

5 measures/120ml/4fl oz/½ cup
    chilled tonic water or
    lemonade

slices of **lime**, to decorate

---

variation

Use fresh apricots or nectarines and
top up with either ginger beer or
ginger ale.

vunderful

A **LONG, LAZY** TIPPLE, CONJURED UP IN THE
HEAT OF ZIMBABWE. LEAVE THE FRUITS IN
THE GIN FOR AS LONG AS POSSIBLE.

method

SERVES 20

1 Strain the lychees from the syrup, if using canned lychees, and place
them in a wide-necked jar with the peach slices and the gin. Leave
overnight or for up to a month.

2 Drain and reserve the gin-soaked lychees and peaches. Mix for each
person, in a large bar glass or jug, 1 measure/25ml/1½ tbsp lychee
gin with 1 measure/25ml/1½ tbsp Pimms and add bitters to taste.

3 Strain into tall tumblers filled with ice cubes.

4 Add chilled tonic water or lemonade, to taste.

5 Put some of the drained, gin-soaked lychees and peaches into the
bottom of each glass and add a muddler, with which to stir and crush
the fruit into the drink.

6 Add a half slice of lime to the rim of each glass and serve.

mai tai

A **VERY REFRESHING,** BUT STRONG, PARTY DRINK THAT **SLIPS DOWN EASILY**.

method

SERVES 1

1 Add the white and dark rum and apricot brandy to a cocktail shaker half full of cracked ice.

ingredients

1 measure/25ml/1½ tbsp
white rum
1 measure/25ml/1½ tbsp
dark rum
1 measure/25ml/1½ tbsp
apricot brandy
3 measures/70ml/4½ tbsp
orange juice, chilled
3 measures/70ml/4½ tbsp
pineapple juice, chilled
1 measure/25ml/1½ tbsp
grenadine

2 Add the well-chilled orange and pineapple juices.

3 Shake together well for about 20 seconds, or until the outside of the cocktail shaker feels cold. Strain into a tumbler of ice.

4 Slowly pour the grenadine into the glass and it will fall to the bottom of the drink to make a glowing red layer,

variation
Mix bitters, rum, orgeat (almond and orange flower water) syrup or almond essence into 300ml/½ pint/1¼ cups orange juice.

sangria

TESTAMENT TO THE **SPANISH** INFLUENCE ON **MEXICAN** COOKING, THIS POPULAR **THIRST-QUENCHER** IS OFTEN SERVED IN LARGE **JUGS**, WITH **ICE** AND **CITRUS** FRUIT SLICES FLOATING ON TOP.

ingredients

750ml/1¼ pints/3 cups **dry red wine**
juice of 2 **limes**
120ml/4fl oz/½ cup freshly squeezed **orange juice**
120ml/4fl oz/½ cup **brandy**
50g/2oz/¼ cup **sugar**
1 **lime** or **lemon**, sliced to decorate
ice, to serve

method

SERVES 6

1 Combine the wine, lime juice, orange juice and brandy in a large glass jug (pitcher).

2 Stir in the sugar until it has dissolved completely.

3 Serve in tall glasses with ice. Decorate each glass with a slice of lime or lemon.

variation
This drink can be made with a 400g/14oz can of chopped tomatoes and tastes almost as good as when made with fresh tomatoes

sangrita

SIPPING SANGRITA AND **TEQUILA** ALTERNATELY IS A **TASTE SENSATION** NOT TO BE MISSED, THE **WARM** FLAVOURS OF THE FIRST **BALANCING** THE **HARSHNESS** OF THE SECOND. THE DRINKS ARE OFTEN SERVED WITH **ANTOJITOS** (NIBBLES) IN MEXICO AS AN **APPETIZER**.

ingredients

450g/1lb ripe **tomatoes**
1 small **onion**, finely chopped
2 small fresh **green fresno chillies**, seeded and chopped
5 measures/120ml/4fl oz/½ cup juice from freshly squeezed **oranges**
juice of 3 **limes**
2.5ml/½ teaspoon **sugar**
pinch of **salt**
1 small shot glass of **golden** or **aged tequila** per person

method

SERVES 8

1 cut a cross in the bottom or each tomato. Place the tomatoes in a heatproof bowl and pour in boiling water to cover. Leave for 3 minutes.

2 LIft the tomatoes out on a slotted spoon and plunge them into a second bowl of cold water. The skins will have begun to peel back from the crosses. Remove the skins, then cut the tomatoes in half and scoop out the seeds with a teaspoon.

3 Chop the tomato flesh and put in a food processor. Add the onion, chillies, orange juice, lime juice, sugar and salt.

4 Process until all the mixture is very smooth then pour into a pitcher and chill for at least 1 hour before serving. Offer each drinker a separate glass of tequila as well. The drinks are sipped alternately.

variation
In some parts of Mexico a less potent but equally refreshing version of sangria is served. Fill tall glasses with ice. Fill each glass two-thirds full with fresh lime juice diluted with water and sweetened with sugar. Fill up with red wine. Tequila is sometimes added to the lime mixture.

ingredients

1 large **pineapple**

50g/2oz **dark brown sugar**

1 litre/1¾ pints/4 cups
blanco tequila

1 **vanilla pod (bean)**

pineapple tequila

MANY **UNIQUE** FLAVOURS HAVE BEEN
DEVELOPED BY **COMBINING** INGREDIENTS
SUCH AS **PINEAPPLE CHUNKS** WITH
BLANCO TEQUILA AND LETTING THEM SIT
FOR A PERIOD OF TIME.

method

SERVES 6

1 Rinse out a large (about 2 litre/3½ pint) wide-necked bottle or
demijohn and sterilize it by placing it in an oven and turning on the
oven to 110°C/225°F/Gas ¼. After 20 minutes remove the bottle from
the oven with oven mitts and leave to cool.

2 Cut the top off the pineapple and then cut away the skin, being careful
to get rid of all the scales. Cut in half, remove the hard centre core
and discard it. Chop the rest of the pineapple into chunks, ensuring
that they are small enough to fit in the bottle neck.

3 When the bottle is completely cold, put the pineapple into the bottle.
Mix the sugar and tequila together in a jug until the sugar dissolves
and then pour into the bottle. Split the vanilla pod and add it to the
rest of the ingredients.

4 Gently agitate the bottle a few times each day to stir the contents. Let
the tequila stand for at least 1 week before drinking. When it has all
been drunk, the pineapple can be used in desserts such as ice cream
or warmed with butter and cinnamon and served with cream.

mango & peach margarita

ADDING PURÉED FRUIT TO THE **CLASSIC** TEQUILA MIXTURE ALTERS THE CONSISTENCY AND MAKES FOR A **GLORIOUS** DRINK THAT RESEMBLES A MILKSHAKE BUT **PACKS** CONSIDERABLY **MORE PUNCH**.

ingredients

2 **mangoes**, peeled and sliced

3 **peaches**, peeled and sliced

5 measures/120ml/4fl oz/
   ½ cup **tequila**

60ml/4 tbsp/2⅔ measures
   triple sec

60ml/4 tbsp/2⅔ measures freshly
   squeezed **lime juice**

10 ice **cubes**, crushed

mango slices, skin on,
   to decorate

method

1 Place the mango and peach slices in a food processor or blender. Process or blend until the fruit is finely chopped. Scrape down the sides of the goblet and blend again until the purée is smooth.

2 Add the tequila, triple sec and lime juice, process or blend for a few seconds, then add the ice. Process or blend again until the drink has the consistency of a milkshake.

3 Pour into cocktail glasses, decorate with the mango slices and serve.

shorts

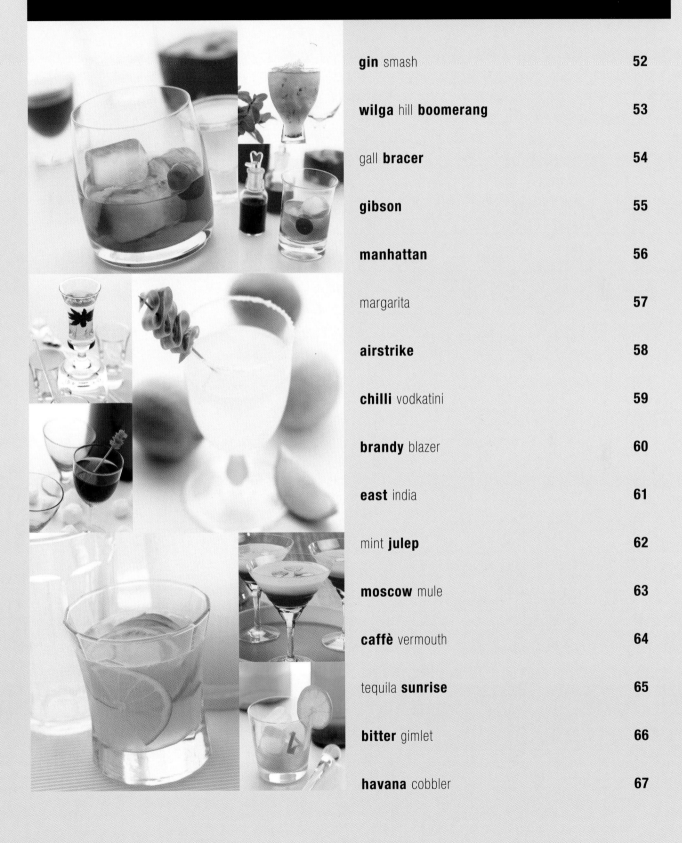

ingredients

15ml/1 tbsp **caster
(superfine) sugar**

4 fresh sprigs of **mint**

2 rneasures/45ml/3 tbsp **dry gin**

---

variation
Use Southern Comfort or bourbon in place of the gin.

gin smash

THIS **SIMPLE** AND VERY **REFRESHING** COCKTAIL CAN BE MADE WITH FRESH **PEPPERMINT**, APPLE MINT OR **BLACK MINT** TO PRODUCE THREE **UNIQUELY FLAVOURED** DRINKS. USE THE VARIETY OF MINT YOU PREFER.

method

SERVES 1

1 Dissolve the sugar in a little water in the cocktail shaker.

2 Place some ice cubes in a clean dishtowel and crush them finely

3 Add the mint to the cocktail shaker and, using a muddler, bruise and press the juices out of the mint.

4 Half fill the shaker with the cracked ice and add the gin.

5 Put the top on the shaker and shake the cocktail for about 20 seconds, to mix the gin with the mint.

6 Strain the cocktail into a small wine glass filled with crushed ice. If you prefer, add fresh mint sprigs and drinking straws.

wilga hill boomerang

THIS **SUNDOWNER** IS MIXED IN A BAR GLASS HALF FULL OF ICE CUBES, AND IS SERVED **SUPER COLD**.

variation

Drop the apple juice and serve over the rocks or, if you prefer, substitute bourbon or Southern Comfort for the gin.

ingredients

1 measure/25ml/1½ tbsp **gin**

¼ measure/5ml/1 tsp **dry vermouth**

¼ measure/5ml/1 tsp **sweet vermouth**

1 measure/25ml/1½ tbsp **clear apple juice**

dash **angostura bitters**

2 dashes **maraschino cherry juice**

strip of **orange rind** and a **maraschino cherry**, to decorate

method

SERVES 1

1 Pour the gin, dry vermouth, sweet vermouth and clear apple juice into a bar glass half-filled with ice, and stir until the outside of the glass has frosted.

2 Add the angostura bitters and maraschino cherry juice to the bottom of a shorts tumbler and add ice cubes

3 Strain the gin and vermouths into the shorts tumbler.

4 Add the strip of orange rind and maraschino cherry and serve.

ingredients

2 dashes **angostura bitters**

2 dashes **grenadine**

2 measures/45ml/3 tbsp **whisky**

lemon rind

maraschino cherry, to
    decorate (optional)

gall bracer

SHORT AND SMART, THIS DRINK IS SERVED
ON THE ROCKS, IN A TUMBLER **FOR A MAN**
OR IN A **DELICATE** LONG-STEMMED
COCKTAIL GLASS, WITH A **MARASCHINO**
CHERRY, **FOR A LADY**.

---

variation
For a longer drink, top up with soda or sparkling mineral water, or for a cocktail
called a Gall Trembler substitute gin for the whisky and add more bitters.

---

method

SERVES 1

1 Half fill a bar glass with ice. Add the angostura bitters, grenadine and
whisky and stir well to chill.

2 Place some ice in a short tumbler and pour the cocktail over it.

3 Holding the lemon rind between the fingers, squeeze out the oils and
juices into the cocktail. Discard the lemon rind.

4 Add a cherry, if you like.

gibson

WELL LOVED IN **JAPAN**, THIS IS A VERSION OF THE MARTINI WITH A **SMALL WHITE ONION** IN IT, RATHER THAN A TWIST OF LEMON. YOU MAY PREFER A HIGHER PROPORTION OF **GIN**.

variation
Add a touch more dry vermouth and a twist of lemon and you have an Australian Kangaroo.

ingredients

½ measure/10ml/2 tsp
extra-dry vermouth
scant 1 measure/20ml/4 tsp
extra-dry gin
2 **pearl onions**, to decorate

method   SERVES 1

1 Pour the vermouth into a bar glass of ice, stir briskly and then pour out. Only the vermouth that clings to the ice and glass should be used.

2 Add the gin and stir for at least 30 seconds, to chill well.

3 Strain into a martini glass either on the rocks or straight up.

4 Thread the pearl onions on to a cocktail stick and add to the drink.

ingredients

2 measures/45ml/3 tbsp
rye whisky

¼ measure/5ml/1 tsp dry
French vermouth

¼ measure/5ml/1 tsp sweet
Italian vermouth

lemon rind and a **maraschino cherry**, to decorate

---

variation

Create a skyscraper by adding a dash of angostura bitters, a teaspoon of maraschino cherry juice, and top up with ginger ale.

manhattan

WHEN MAKING MANHATTANS IT'S A MATTER OF **PREFERENCE** WHETHER YOU USE **SWEET** VERMOUTH, **DRY** VERMOUTH OR A **MIXTURE**. BOTH OF THE FORMER REQUIRE A DASH OF **ANGOSTURA BITTERS**.

method

SERVES 1

1 Pour the whisky and vermouths into a bar glass filled with ice. Stir well for about 30 seconds, to mix and chill.

2 Strain, on the rocks or straight up, into a chilled cocktail glass.

3 Using a canelle knife, pare away a small strip of lemon rind. Tie it into a knot, to help release the oils from the rind, and drop it into the cocktail.

4 To finish, add a maraschino cherry with its stalk left intact.

margarita

TRADITIONALLY THIS POPULAR **STRONG** APERITIF IS MADE WITH **TEQUILA** AND **COINTREAU**, BUT IT IS ALSO GOOD MADE WITH **VODKA** AND **TRIPLE SEC** (A TERM USED FOR **WHITE CURAÇAO**).

method

SERVES 1

1 Rub the rim of the glass with a wedge of fresh lime.

ingredients

1 measure/25ml/1½ tbsp
  tequilla
1 measure/25ml/1½ tbsp
  Cointreau
⅔ measure/15ml/1 tbsp
  lime juice
wedge of fresh **lime**, fine **salt** crystals and **cucumber** peel, to decorate

variation
Replace the Cointreau with blue curaçao for an interesting colour and flavour.

2 Invert the glass into fine salt crystals, to create a rim of salt. Turn the glass the right way up and chill until required.

3 Pour the tequilla and Cointreau, with the lime juice, into a cocktail shaker filled with ice. Shake for 20 seconds.

4 Carefully strain the cocktail into the frosted glass.

5 Using a sharp knife or vegetable peeler, cut a long thin strip of green peel from a whole cucumber.

6 Trim the cucumber peel to size and thread it on to a cocktail stick. Add to the glass to decorate.

ingredients

2 measures/45ml/3 tbsp
Galliano

1 measure/25ml/1½ tbsp **brandy**

1 **star anise**

airstrike

A VARIATION ON A **VAL D'ISÈRE** SHOOTER,
AN **AIRSTRIKE** IS A SIMILAR IDEA TO THE
ITALIAN **FLAMING SAMBUCCA.**

method
SERVES 1

1 Put the Galliano and brandy in a small saucepan and heat very gently,
until just warm.

2 Carefully pour into a heat-resistant glass standing on a small plate or
saucer; add the star anise.

3 Using a lighted taper or long match, pass the flame over the surface
of the drink to ignite it. The flame will be low and very pale, so be
careful not to burn yourself.

4 Leave to burn for a couple of minutes, until the star anise has sizzled
a little and released extra aroma into the drink. Leave to cool slightly
before drinking. The top of the glass will be hot!

---

variation
Use all Sambucca and float two or three coffee beans on the surface instead of
the star anise before lighting.

---

chilli vodkatini

NOT QUITE A **MARTINI**, BUT ALMOST. OVER THE YEARS THE PROPORTIONS OF **VODKA TO VERMOUTH** HAVE VARIED WIDELY, WITH THE VODKA BECOMING ALMOST **OVERWHELMING**. BE SURE TO HAVE YOUR **CHILLI VODKA** MADE WELL IN ADVANCE AND READY TO USE.

method   SERVES 1

1 Add the chilli vodka to a bar glass filled with ice and mix for about 30 seconds, until the outside of the glass has frosted.

2 Add the vermouth to a chilled cocktail glass and swirl it round the inside of the glass, to moisten it. Discard any remaining vermouth.

3 Cut one of the pickled chillies in half and discard the seeds. Stuff the pitted green olive with the chilli.

4 Thread the stuffed olive on to a cocktail stick, together with the remaining chilli.

5 Strain the cocktail into the prepared cocktail glass.

6 Add the olive and chilli decoration to the drink before serving.

ingredients

1 measure/25ml/l½ tbsp
  chilli vodka
¼ measure/5ml/l tsp medium or
  dry **French vermouth**
2 small **pickled** or **vodka-soaked chillies**, to decorate
1 **pitted green olive**,
  to decorate

variation
For the classic Martini, use gin, but serve with a twist of lemon. Mix plain vodka and dry vermouth for a Vodka Martini. Add an olive and it becomes a Vodka Gibson.

ingredients

½ **orange**

1 **lemon**

2 measures/45ml/3 tbsp **cognac**

1 **sugar cube**

½ measure/10ml/2 tsp **Kahlúa**

pieces of **orange rind**, threaded
on to a cocktail stick, to
decorate

---

variation

Pour the hot cognac and Kahlúa
mix on to freshly brewed coffee
and serve.

brandy blazer

A **WARMING** AFTER-DINNER TIPPLE, IDEAL
SERVED WITH FRESH VANILLA **ICE CREAM**
OR **CARAMELIZED** ORANGES.

method   SERVES 1

1 Thinly pare the rind from the orange and lemon, removing and
discarding as much of the white pith as possible.

2 Put the cognac, sugar cube, lemon and orange rind in a small pan.

3 Heat gently, then remove from the heat, light a match and pass the
flame close to the surface of the liquid. The alcohol will burn with a
low, blue flame for about a minute, so be careful not to burn yourself.
Blow out the flame.

4 Add the Kahlúa to the pan and strain into a heat resistant liqueur
glass. Decorate with the cocktail stick threaded with orange rind. Let it
cool slightly and serve warm.

east india

THIS **SHORT AND ELEGANT** DRINK CAN BE
SERVED AS AN **APERITIF**, DRESSED WITH A
TWIST OF **LIME** RIND AND DECORATED WITH
A **MARASCHINO CHERRY**.

---
variation
Mix equal quantities of dry vermouth and dry sherry with angostura bitters and
serve on the rocks.
---

ingredients

⅔ measure/15ml/1 tbsp **brandy**

2 dashes **white curaçao**

2 dashes **pineapple juice**

2 dashes **angostura bitters**

1 **lime** and a **maraschino
    cherry**, to decorate

method

SERVES 1

1 Put the brandy, curaçao, pineapple juice and bitters into a bar glass
filled with ice.

2 Stir the cocktail well for about 20 seconds until chilled and strain into
a squat tumbler over the rocks.

3 Using a canelle knife, remove a piece of rind from a lime.

4 Tightly twist into a coil, hold for a few seconds, and add to the drink
with a maraschino cherry.

ingredients

15ml/1 tbsp **caster
(superfine) sugar**
8–10 fresh **mint leaves**
15ml/l tbsp **hot water**
2 measures/45ml/3 tbsp
bourbon or **whisky**

mint julep

ONE OF THE **OLDEST COCKTAILS**, THIS
ORIGINATED IN THE **SOUTHERN STATES OF
AMERICA.** ADD FRESH MINT LEAVES
ACCORDING TO TASTE.

method   SERVES 1

1 Pace the sugar in a pestle and mortar, or in a bar glass with a
muddler. Tear the mint leaves into small pieces and add to the sugar.

2 Bruise the mint leaves to release their flavour and colour.

3 Add the hot water to the mint leaves and grind well together.

4 Spoon into a snifter glass or brandy balloon and half fill with some
crushed ice.

5 Add the bourbon or whisky to the snifter glass.

6 Stir until the outside of the glass has frosted. Allow to stand for a
couple of minutes, to let the ice melt slightly and dilute the drink.
Serve with straws, if you prefer.

---
variation
Add a dash of chilled soda for a refreshing long drink.
---

moscow mule

method

ONE OF THE **CLASSIC AMERICAN** VODKA-BASED COCKTAILS, WHICH USES A LARGE QUANTITY OF **ANGOSTURA** BITTERS FOR ITS **FLAVOUR** AND COLOUR AND **ENOUGH VODKA** TO GIVE THE DRINK **A REAL KICK**.

1 Pour the vodka, bitters, lime cordial and lime juice into a bar glass filled with ice. Mix together well.

2 Strain into a tumbler containing a couple of ice cubes.

3 Top up the mixture, to taste, with ginger beer.

4 Add a few halved slices of lime to the cocktail before serving.

variation
For a Malawi Shandy, mix ice-cold ginger beer with a dash of bitters and top up with soda water. Of course, the vodka does not have to be left out.

ingredients

2 measures/45ml/3 tbsp **vodka**

6 dashes **angostura bitters**

dash **lime cordial**

½ measure/10 ml/2 tsp
   lime juice

3 measures/70 ml/4½ tbsp
   ginger beer

slices of **lime**, to decorate

ingredients

5 measures/120ml/4fl oz/½ cup
red vermouth

2⅔ measures/60ml/4 tbsp very
strong cold **coffee**

250ml/8fl oz/1 cup **milk**

30ml/2 tbsp **crushed ice**

10ml/2 tsp **sugar**

coffee beans, to decorate

---
tip
To make very strong coffee use

caffè vermouth

VERMOUTH IS NOT AN OBVIOUS CHOICE TO
PARTNER COFFEE, BUT THE RESULTING
FLAVOUR IS GOOD; **DIFFERENT** AND
SOPHISTICATED. USE A LITTLE LESS IF
UNSURE OF THE FLAVOUR.

method
SERVES 2

1 In a cocktail shaker, combine all the ingredients and shake well.

2 Serve immediately in cocktail glasses or glass tumblers. Decorate with
a few roasted coffee beans.

---
variation
Different flavours and textures can be obtained by varying the type of milk used,
or by using a little cream instead of milk for a richer version.
---

tequila sunrise

THIS DRINK TAKES ITS NAME FROM THE WAY THE **GRENADINE** – A BRIGHT RED **CORDIAL** MADE FROM **POMEGRANATE** JUICE – FIRST **SINKS** IN THE GLASS OF **ORANGE JUICE** AND **THEN RISES** TO THE SURFACE.

method

SERVES 1

1 Half fill a cocktail glass with crushed ice. Pour in the tequila, then the orange and lime juices, which should be freshly squeezed. Don't be tempted to use concentrated orange juice from a carton or bottled lime juice, or the flavour of the finished drink will be spoiled.

2 Quickly add the grenadine, pouring it down the back of a teaspoon held in the glass so that it sinks to the bottom of the drink and serve immediately.

ingredients

1 measure/25ml/1½ tbsp
   golden tequila
2⅔ measures/60ml/4 tbsp freshly
   squeezed **orange juice**
juice of 1 **lime**
5ml/1 tsp **grenadine**

variation
To make a Pink Cadillac, use Grand Marnier instead of orange juice.

ingredients

1 **lime**, cut into wedges

1 measure/25ml/1½ tbsp **gin**

2 dashes **angostura bitters**

slice and rind of **lime**, to decorate

bitter gimlet

A **CLASSIC APERITIF**, WHICH COULD EASILY
BE TURNED INTO A REFRESHING LONGER
DRINK BY TOPPING UP WITH **CHILLED TONIC**
OR SODA WATER.

method

SERVES 1

1 Place the lime at the bottom of the bar glass and, using a muddler,
press the juice out of the lime.

2 Add cracked ice, the gin and the bitters and stir well, until cold.

3 Strain the cocktail into a short tumbler over ice cubes.

4 Add a triangle of lime rind to the drink and use a slice of lime to
decorate the rim of the glass.

---

variation

Add a teaspoon of sugar, for a sweeter version, or add a dash or two of
crème de menthe to create a fallen angel.

---

havana cobbler

A VERY **SWEET** DRINK THAT IS SURPRISINGLY **REFRESHING** WHEN SERVED IN HOT WEATHER.

variation

Cobblers can be made with brandy, gin and sherry or even wine or champagne; for the latter, naturally, don't shake it and omit the port!

ingredients

5ml/1 tsp **sugar syrup**
½ measure/10ml/2 tsp **green ginger wine**
1 measure/25ml/1½ tbsp **Cuban or white rum**
1 measure/25ml/1½ tbsp **port**

method

SERVES 1

1 Put the sugar syrup and ginger wine in a cocktail shaker, half filled with ice. Add the white rum.

2 Shake together for 20 seconds.

3 Strain the cocktail into a chilled short tumbler.

4 Tilt the glass and slowly pour the port down the side of the glass to form a layer floating on top of the cocktail.

non-alcoholic

ingredients

2 **pineapples**

juice of 2 **limes**

475ml/16fl oz/2 cups **still mineral water**

50g/2oz/¼ cup **caster (superfine) sugar**

ice cubes, to serve

tip

When peeling a pineapple cut off the top and bottom and remove the skin with a spiral action, cutting deeply enough to remove most of the "eyes". Any remaining "eyes" can be cut out using a small knife.

pineapple & lime agua fresca

THE **VIVID COLOURS** OF THIS FRESH FRUIT DRINK GIVE SOME INDICATION OF ITS **WONDERFUL FLAVOUR**. IT MAKES A DELICIOUS MIDDAY **REFRESHER** OR PICK-ME-UP AT THE END OF A HARD DAY.

method

SERVES 4

1 Peel the pineapples and chop the flesh, removing the core and "eyes". You should have about 450g/1lb flesh. Put this in a food processor or blender and add the lime juice and half the mineral water. Purée to a smooth pulp. Stop the machine and scrape the mixture from the side of the goblet once or twice during processing.

2 Place a sieve over a large bowl. Tip the pineapple pulp into the sieve and press it through with a wooden spoon. Pour the sieved mixture into a large jug (pitcher), cover and chill for about 1 hour.

3 Stir in the remaining mineral water and sugar to taste. Serve with ice.

tamarind agua fresca

TAMARIND, SOMETIMES REFERRED TO AS THE **INDIAN DATE**, IS NATIVE TO **ASIA** AND **NORTH AFRICA**. IT IS USED MEDICINALLY AND AS AN **ANTISEPTIC**. THE FRUIT HAS A SWEET-SOUR TASTE AND MAKES A DRINK SIMILAR TO **LEMONADE**.

method

SERVES 4

1 Pour the water into a pan and heat until warm. Remove from the heat and pour into a bowl. Peel the tamarind pods and add the pulp to the warm water. Soak for at least 4 hours.

2 Place a sieve over a clean bowl. Pour the tamarind pulp and water into the sieve, then press the pulp through the sieve with the back of a wooden spoon, leaving the black seeds behind. Discard the seeds.

3 Add the sugar to the tamarind mixture and stir well until dissolved. Pour into a jug and chill thoroughly before serving in tumblers filled with ice.

ingredients

1 litre/1¾ pints/4 cups **water**
225g/8oz **tamarind pods**
25g/1oz/2 tbsp **caster (superfine) sugar**
ice cubes, to serve

tip
Jars of tamarind pulp or paste are sold at Indian food shops and Oriental stores. The dried pulp is also sold in solid blocks. All these products need soaking and sieving, but you will be spared the time-consuming task of peeling the pods.

ingredients

1 **lemon**

dash **angostura bitters**

2 measures/45ml/3 tbsp
   raspberry, **Orange Pekoe** or
   Assam tea, chilled (optional)

1 measure/25ml/1½ tbsp clear,
   unsweetened **apple juice**

5 measures/120ml/4fl oz/½ cup
   dry **ginger ale** or **lemonade**

horse's fall

A **LONG, REFRESHING DRINK** TO SERVE ON
A HOT SUMMER'S DAY. THE TYPE OF TEA IS A
MATTER OF **TASTE** AND PREFERENCE.

method

SERVES 1

1 Cut the peel from the lemon in one continuous strip and use to line
   and decorate a long cocktail glass. Chill the glass until required.

2 Add a dash of angostura bitters to the bottom of the glass.

3 Measure the tea, if using, into the cocktail shaker and add the
   apple juice.

4 Shake everything together for about 20 seconds.

5 Strain into the prepared, chilled cocktail glass.

6 Top up with chilled ginger ale or lemonade to taste.

---

variation

Substitute calvados or brandy for the flavoured tea for a Horse's Neck.

---

sunburst

BURSTING WITH **FRESHNESS** AND VITAMINS, THIS DRINK IS A GOOD EARLY MORNING **PICK-ME-UP**.

method

SERVES 2

1 Place the apple, carrots and mango in a blender or food processor and process to a pulp.

ingredients

1 green **apple**, cored and
   chopped
3 **carrots**, peeled and chopped
1 **mango**, peeled and stoned
7 measures/150ml/¼ pint//⅔ cup
   freshly squeezed **orange**
   juice, chilled
6 **strawberries**, hulled
slice of **orange**, to decorate

2 Add the orange juice and strawberries and process again.

3 If you prefer, strain through a sieve, pressing out all the juice with the back of a wooden spoon. Discard any pulp left in the sieve.

4 Pour into tumblers filled with ice cubes and serve immediately, decorated with a slice of orange.

variation
Any combination of fruit juice and yogurt can be shaken together. Try natural yogurt with apple, apricot and mango.

ingredients

115g/4oz **Galia**, **honeydew** or
    watermelon
5 small **red grapes**
3 measures/70ml/4½ tbsp
    unsweetened **red grape juice**

To decorate
red grapes
1 **egg white**, lightly beaten
15g/½ oz **caster**
    (superfine) sugar

variation
For a longer fizzy drink, top up the
melon and grape purée with equal
quantities of grape juice and tonic or
soda water.

scarlet lady

WITH ITS **FRESH AND FRUITY** TONES, THIS
DRINK COULD EASILY PASS AS AN ALCOHOLIC
WINE-BASED COCKTAIL.

method
SERVES 1

1 To make the decoration, dip the red grapes into the egg white and roll
in the sugar.

2 For the cocktail, put the melon and grapes in a blender and process
until they form a smooth purée.

3 Add the red grape juice and continue to process for another minute.

4 Strain the juice into a bar glass of ice and stir until chilled.

5 Pour into a chilled cocktail glass and decorate with the sugar-frosted
grapes threaded on to a cocktail stick.

virgin prairie oyster

A **SUPERIOR** PICK-ME-UP AND A **VARIATION** ON THE **BLOODY** AND **VIRGIN MARY**. THE TOMATO BASE CAN BE DRUNK WITHOUT THE RAW **EGG YOLK**, IF IT DOES NOT APPEAL TO YOU. USE ONLY **FRESH** FREE-RANGE EGGS.

ingredients

175ml/6fl oz/¾ cup
tomato juice
10ml/2 tsp
Worcestershire sauce
5–10ml/1–2 tsp
balsamic vinegar
1 **egg yolk**
cayenne pepper,
to taste

method

SERVES 1

1 Measure the tomato juice into a large bar glass and stir over plenty of ice, until well chilled.

2 Strain into a tall tumbler half filled with ice cubes.

3 Add the Worcestershire sauce and balsamic vinegar, to taste, and use a swizzle stick to mix together.

4 Float the egg yolk on top and lightly dust with cayenne pepper.

ingredients

1 **cooking apple**

1 **orange**, scrubbed

1 **lemon**, scrubbed

20 whole **cloves**

7.5cm/3in fresh root
ginger, peeled

25g/1oz **soft brown sugar**

350ml/12fl oz/1½ cups
bitter lemon or
non-alcoholic wine

wedges of **orange** rind and whole
cloves, to decorate

fruit and ginger ale

THIS DRINK CAN BE MADE WITH READY-
SQUEEZED **APPLE** AND **ORANGE JUICES**,
BUT **ROASTING** THE FRUIT WITH **CLOVES**
GIVES A MUCH BETTER **FLAVOUR**.

method   SERVES 4–6

1 Preheat the oven to 200°C/400°F/Gas 6. Score the apple around the middle and stud the orange and lemon with the cloves. Bake them in the oven for 25 minutes until soft and completely cooked through.

2 Quarter the orange and lemon and pulp the apple, discarding the skin and the core. Finely grate the ginger. Place the fruit and ginger together in a bowl with the soft brown sugar.

3 Add 300ml/½ pint/1¼ cups boiling water. Using a spoon, squeeze the fruit to release more flavour. Cover and leave to cool for an hour or overnight.

4 Strain into a jug of cracked ice and use a spoon to press out all the juices from the fruit. Add the bitter lemon or non-alcoholic wine, to taste. Decorate with an orange rind studded with cloves, threaded on to a cocktail stick.

licuardo de melon

AMONG THE MOST **REFRESHING** DRINKS TO MAKE ARE FRUIT EXTRACTS MIXED WITH **HONEY** AND CHILLED WATER.

method

SERVES 4

1 Cut the watermelon flesh into chunks, cutting away the skin and discarding the shiny black seeds.

2 Place the chunks in a large bowl, pour over the chilled water and leave to stand for 10 minutes.

3 Tip the mixture into a large sieve set over a bowl. Using a wooden spoon, press gently on the fruit to extract all the liquid.

4 Stir in the lime juice and sweeten to taste with honey.

5 Pour into a jug, add ice cubes and stir. Serve in tumblers.

ingredients

1 **watermelon**
1 litre/1¾ pints/4 cups chilled **water**
juice of 2 **limes**
honey, to taste
ice cubes, to serve

ingredients

2 measures/45ml/3 tbsp
lime cordial

2–3 dashes **angostura bitters**

7 measures/150ml/¼ pint/
⅔ cup chilled **tonic water**

frozen slices of **lime**, to decorate

decorative **ice cubes**, to serve

volunteer

THIS IS AN IDEAL PICK-ME-UP OR **NON-ALCOHOLIC** DRINK FOR THE CHOSEN DRIVER AT A **PARTY**. IT WAS **DEVISED** AND **DRUNK** DURING A VERY ROUGH **CHANNEL** CROSSING IN TOO SMALL A BOAT!

method

SERVES 1

1 Place the lime cordial at the bottom of the glass and shake in the angostura bitters, according to taste.

2 Add a few decorative ice cubes to the glass, if liked.

3 Top up with tonic water and add the frozen lime slices.

---

variation
Use fresh lime or grapefruit juice and a splash of sugar syrup instead of the lime cordial, and top up with ginger ale.

---

steel works

A **THIRST-QUENCHING** DRINK, WHICH IS IDEAL TO SERVE AT ANY TIME OF THE **DAY OR NIGHT.**

variation
For a Rock Shandy, pour equal quantities of lemonade and soda on to bitters or use your favourite variety of the naturally flavoured and unsweetened fruit cordials.

ingredients

2 measures/45ml/3 tbsp
passion-fruit cordial
dash **angostura bitters**
3 measures/70ml/4½ tbsp soda
water, chilled
3 measures/70ml/4½ tbsp
lemonade, chilled
1 **passion fruit** (optional)

method

1 Pour the passion-fruit cordial straight into a long tumbler. Add the angostura bitters to the glass and then add some ice cubes.

2 Top up the drink with the chilled soda water and lemonade and stir briefly together.

3 Cut the passion fruit in half, if using; scoop the seeds and flesh from the fruit and add to the drink. Stir the drink gently before serving.

ingredients

rind and juice of 2 **oranges**

rind and juice of 1 **lemon**

15g/½oz **caster**
(superfine) sugar,
or to taste

75ml/5 tbsp **water**

slices of **orange** and **lemon**,
to decorate

variation

The same principle can be used to
make pineapple, peach, grape and
soft fruit juices, but sweeten with
sugar syrup. These will keep in the
refrigerator for 2–3 days.

st clements

FRESHLY SQUEEZED ORANGE AND LEMON
JUICE CREATES A SIMPLE BUT **THIRST-**
QUENCHING DRINK.

method

SERVES 1

1 Wash the oranges and lemons and then thinly pare off the rind from
the fruit with a sharp knife, leaving the white pith behind. Remove the
pith from the fruit and discard it.

2 Put the fruit rind in a pan, with the sugar and water. Heat gently over a
low heat and stir gently until the sugar has dissolved.

3 Remove the pan from the heat and press the orange and lemon rind
against the sides of the pan to release all their oils. Cover the pan and
cool. Remove and discard the rind.

4 Purée the oranges and lemon and sweeten the fruit pulp by adding the
cooled citrus syrup over the fruit pulp. Leave aside for 2–3 hours for
the flavours to infuse.

5 Sieve the fruit pulp, pressing the solids in the sieve to extract as much
of the juice as possible.

6 Pour into a tall glass filled with finely crushed ice and decorate with a
slice of orange and lemon.

bandrek

A **RICH AND CREAMY** VERSION OF THE **SPICY** INDONESIAN DRINK. SERVE WARM OR CHILLED. IF YOU LIKE, ADD A **VERY FRESH** EGG TO THE SYRUP AND MILKS IN THE BLENDER AND YOU'LL HAVE AN EGGNOG.

method

SERVES 4

1 Put the cloves, juniper berries, cinnamon, cardamom pods and peppercorns, with the sugar cube, in a saucepan. Heat gently to release the aroma and flavours of the spices.

2 Add the water and bring to the boil.

3 Continue to boil for 10 minutes or until reduced to 30–45ml/ 2–3 tbsp of spicy flavoured syrup. Remove from the heat and cool.

4 Pour the syrup into a blender with the coconut milk and whole milk and process until smooth.

5 Strain over cracked ice into a stemmed glass.

6 Decorate with cinnamon sticks and a maraschino cherry.

variation
Stir   measure/10ml/2 tsp whisky into the finished drink or add the strained spiced syrup to double-strength black coffee. Process in a blender with a little double cream, strain and serve over ice.

ingredients

3 whole **cloves**

3 **juniper berries**, bruised

cinnamon stick

6 **green cardamom pods**,
    bruised

4 whole **black peppercorns**

1 **sugar cube**

175ml/6fl oz/¾ cup **water**

2 measures/45ml/3 tbsp
    coconut milk

3 measures/70 ml/4½ tbsp
    full-fat (whole) milk

cinnamon sticks and a
    maraschino cherry,
    to decorate

ingredients

350ml/12fl oz/1½ cups cold
   black coffee
350ml/12fl oz/1½ cups
   natural (plain) yogurt
20 ml/4 tsp **sugar**
a pinch of ground **cinnamon**,
   to decorate

coffee yogurt

THIS IS REALLY A **VARIATION** ON A
"LASSI", THE REFRESHING **YOGURT** DRINK
OF **INDIAN** RESTAURANTS. IT CAN BE MADE
AS EITHER A **SWEET** DRINK (TRADITIONALLY
WITH **SUGAR** AND GROUND **CINNAMON**) **OR**
SALTY (USING SALT AND A LITTLE **CUMIN**).

method

SERVES 2

1 Combine all the ingredients in a blender. Mix until creamy.

2 Serve sprinkled with cinnamon.

variation
For a salty version, use 5ml/1 tsp salt and a pinch of ground cumin, instead of
the cinnamon, possibly with some sugar to taste, if desired.

chilled coffee caribbean

USE **COFFEE** THAT IS NOT TOO STRONG; FILTER COFFEE GIVES AN IDEAL **CLEAN**, **CLEAR TEXTURE.**

method

1 Add the cooled coffee to the fruit slices in a large bowl.

2 Stir and chill in the freezer for about 1 hour or until very cold.

3 Remove from the freezer and stir again. Remove the fruit slices from the liquid. Add sugar to taste, and stir in the bitters, if using.

4 Add three ice cubes per drink to tall glasses, or whisky tumblers, then pour over the chilled coffee drink. Decorate with a half-slice of orange or lemon on the rim or add to the drink, if you prefer.

ingredients

600ml/2½ cups/1 pint strong filter
  coffee, cooled for about
  20 minutes
½ **orange** and ½ **lemon**,
  thinly sliced
1 **pineapple** slice
sugar, to taste
1–2 drops **angostura bitters**
  (optional)
slices of **orange** or **lemon**,
  to decorate

icy cool

ingredients

mixture of small edible **berries**
   or **currants**
pieces of thinly pared **lemon** or
   orange rind
tiny **edible flowers**
4 scoops of **lemon sorbet**
30ml/2 tbsp **gin**
about 120ml/4fl oz/½ cup chilled
   tonic water

tip
When making the ice cubes, choose small herb flowers such as borage or mint, or edible flowers such as rose geraniums, primulas or rose buds.

gin & lemon fizz

IF **GIN AND TONIC** IS YOUR TIPPLE, TRY THIS **CHILLED ALTERNATIVE**. THE FRUIT AND **FLOWER ICE** CUBES MAKE A **LIVELY DECORATION** FOR ANY ICED DRINK.

method

SERVES 2

1 To make the decorated ice cubes, dip each fruit, piece of rind or edible flower in water and then place in a section of an ice cube tray that is half filled with ice. Freeze until firm, then top up the ice cube trays with water and return to the freezer to freeze completely.

2 Divide the sorbet among two cocktail glasses or use small tumblers, with a capacity of about 150ml/ pint/⅔ cup.

3 Spoon over the gin and add a couple of the ornamental ice cubes to each glass. Top up with tonic water and serve immediately.

cranberry, cinnamon & ginger

THE **COMBINATION** OF PARTIALLY FROZEN CRANBERRY AND **APPLE JUICE** IS **WONDERFULLY SLUSHY** AND CONTRIBUTES A REFRESHING **TART, CLEAN FLAVOUR**.

method

SERVES 4

1 Pour the cranberry juice into a shallow freezerproof container and freeze for about 2 hours or until a thick layer of ice crystals has formed around the edges.

2 Mash with a fork to break up the ice, then return the mixture to the freezer for a further 2–3 hours until almost solid.

3 Pour the apple juice into a small saucepan, add 2 cinnamon sticks and bring to just below boiling point. Pour into a jug and leave to cool, then remove the cinnamon sticks and set them aside with the other cinnamon sticks. Chill the juice until it is very cold.

4 Spoon the cranberry ice into a food processor. making sure that it can be used for crushing ice. If not, break the ice into smaller pieces by wrapping in a cloth and pounding with a mallet. Add the apple juice and blend very briefly until slushy.

5 Pile into cocktail glasses or flutes, top up with chilled ginger ale and decorate with the fresh or frozen cranberries. Pop a long cinnamon stick into each glass, to use as a swizzle stick.

ingredients

600ml/1 pint/2½ cups chilled **cranberry juice**

150ml/¼ pint/⅔ cup **clear apple juice**

4 **cinnamon sticks**

about 400ml/14fl oz/1⅔ cups chilled **ginger ale**

a few fresh or frozen **cranberries**, to decorate

variation
As an alternative decoration, thread cranberries on four cocktail sticks and add one to each glass instead of a cinnamon stick.

soft fruit & ginger cup

A COLOURFUL **MEDLEY OF SOFT FRUITS** STEEPED IN VODKA AND **SERVED** WITH AN ICY BLEND OF **SORBET** AND **GINGER ALE**. YOU WILL DEFINITELY **NEED SPOONS** FOR THIS ONE.

ingredients

115g/4oz/1 cup **strawberries**

115g/4oz/⅔ cup **raspberries**, hulled

50g/2oz/½ cup **blueberries**

15ml/1 tbsp **caster (superfine) sugar**

90ml/6 tbsp **vodka**

600ml/1 pint/2½ cups **ginger ale**

4 large scoops of **orange sorbet**

20ml/4 tsp **grenadine**

4 **physalis flowers**, to decorate

method

SERVES 4

1 Hull the strawberries, cut them in half and put them in a bowl with the raspberries, blueberries and sugar. Pour over the vodka and toss lightly. Cover and chill for at least 30 minutes.

2 Put the ginger ale and sorbet in a blender or food processor and process until smooth. Pour into four bowl-shaped glasses and add a couple of ice cubes to each glass of sorbet mixture.

3 Spoon a teaspoon of grenadine over the ice cubes in each glass, then spoon the vodka-steeped fruits on top of the sorbet mixture and ice cubes. Decorate each glass with a physalis. Serve immediately.

> ### variation
> Any combination of soft fruit can be used for this iced drink. Blackberries, for example, would also work well.

sparkling peach melba

THIS **REFRESHING** FRUIT FIZZ IS AN EXCELLENT CHOICE FOR **SUMMER** CELEBRATIONS. AS WITH MOST **SOFT** FRUIT RECIPES, ITS **SUCCESS** DEPENDS ON USING THE **RIPEST, TASTIEST** PEACHES AND **RASPBERRIES** AVAILABLE.

ingredients

3 ripe **peaches**

90ml/6 tbsp **orange juice**

75g/3oz/½ cup **raspberries**

10ml/2 tsp **icing (confectioners') sugar**

about 500ml/17fl oz/2¼ cups **raspberry sorbet**

about 400ml/14fl oz/1⅔ cups **medium sparkling chilled white** wine

fresh **mint** sprigs, to decorate

method

SERVES 4

1 Put the peaches in a heatproof bowl and pour over boiling water to cover. Leave for approximately 1 minute, then drain the peaches and peel off the skins.

2 Cut the fruit in half and remove the stones (pits). Chop the peach halves roughly and purée them with the orange juice in a food processor or blender until smooth. Scrape the purée into a bowl.

3 Put the raspberries in the food processor or blender. Add the icing sugar and process until smooth. Press the raspberry purée through a sieve into a bowl. Chill both purées for at least 1 hour.

4 Spoon the chilled peach purée into four tall glasses.

5 Add scoops of sorbet to come to the top of the glasses. Spoon the raspberry purée around the sorbet.

6 Top up each glass with sparkling wine. Decorate with the mint sprigs and serve.

> ### variation
> When fresh ripe peaches are unavailable, use canned peach halves in juice or light syrup.

ingredients

For the yogurt ice

175g/6oz/¾ cup **caster
    (superfine) sugar**

150ml/¼ pint/⅔ cup **water**

2 **lemons**

500ml/17fl oz/2¼ cups
    **Greek (US strained
    plain) yogurt**

For each drink

120ml/4fl oz/½ cup
    mango juice

2–3 **ice cubes** (optional)

fresh **mint** sprigs and wedges of
    mango, to serve

> ### tip
> Make sure you buy Greek yogurt
> for this drink as it adds a lovely,
> sharp tang.

iced mango lassi

BASED ON A TRADITIONAL **INDIAN** DRINK,
THIS IS EXCELLENT WITH **SPICY FOOD**, OR
AS A WELCOME **COOLER** AT ANY TIME OF
DAY. THE **YOGURT ICE** THAT FORMS THE
BASIS OF THIS DRINK IS A **USEFUL** RECIPE TO
ADD TO YOUR **REPERTOIRE** – IT IS LIGHTER
AND **FRESHER** THAN CREAM-BASED ICES.

method
SERVES 3–4

1 To make the yogurt ice, put the sugar and water in a pan and heat
gently, stirring occasionally, until the sugar has dissolved. Pour the
syrup into a jug. Leave to cool, then chill until very cold.

2 Grate the lemons and then squeeze them. Add the rind and juice to
the chilled syrup and stir well to mix.

3 *by hand*: Pour the syrup mixture into a container and freeze until
thickened. Beat in the yogurt and return to the freezer until thick
enough to scoop.
using an ice cream maker: Churn the mixture until it thickens. Stir in
the yogurt and churn for 2 minutes more until well mixed. Transfer to
a plastic tub or similar freezerproof container and freeze.

4 To make each lassi, briefly blend the mango juice with three small
scoops of the yogurt ice in a food processor or blender until just
smooth. Pour the mixture into a tall glass or tumbler and add the ice
cubes, if using.

5 Top each drink with another scoop of the yogurt ice and decorate.
Serve immediately.

> ### variation
> Add one small chopped banana when blending the ingredients together for a
> substantial summer smoothie.

tropical fruit sodas

FOR MANY **CHILDREN**, SCOOPS OF VANILLA
ICE CREAM, SERVED IN A FROTH OF
LEMONADE WOULD MAKE THE **PERFECT
TREAT**. THIS MORE ELABORATE VERSION
WILL APPEAL TO **ADULTS TOO**.

method

SERVES 4

1 Line a baking sheet with foil. Make four small mounds of sugar on
the foil, using about 2.5ml/ tsp each time and spacing them well
apart. Place under a moderate grill for about 2 minutes until the sugar
mounds have turned to a pale golden caramel.

2 Immediately swirl each pool of caramel with the tip of a cocktail stick
or skewer to give a slightly feathery finish. Leave to cool.

3 Cut the pawpaw in half. Scoop out and discard the seeds, then remove
the skin and chop the flesh. Skin the mango, cut the flesh off the
stone and chop it into bite-size chunks. Mix the pawpaw and mango in
a bowl.

4 Cut each passion fruit in half and scoop the pulp into the bowl of fruit.
Mix well, cover and chill until ready to serve.

5 Divide the chilled fruit mixture among four large tumblers, each with a
capacity of about 300ml/ pint/1 cups.

6 Add one scoop of each type of ice cream to each glass. Peel the
caramel decorations carefully away from the foil and press gently into
the ice cream. Top up with lemonade or soda and serve.

ingredients

10ml/2 tsp **granulated sugar**

1 **pawpaw**

1 small ripe, **mango**

2 **passion fruit**

8 large scoops of classic **vanilla
ice cream**

8 large scoops of **caramel or
toffee ice cream**

about 400ml/14fl oz/1⅔ cups
chilled **lemonade or soda
water**

variations
Use a mixture of strawberries and
raspberries or other more familiar
fruits for children. For adults, a splash
of vodka or kirsch can be added to
the fruits.

snowball

method

FOR MANY OF US, A **"SNOWBALL"** IS A DRINK THAT WE INDULGE IN ONCE OR TWICE AT CHRISTMAS TIME. THIS **ICED VERSION**, ENHANCED WITH MELTING **VANILLA** ICE CREAM, **LIME** AND **NUTMEG**, MAY PROVIDE THE MOTIVATION FOR DRINKING **ADVOCAAT** ON **OTHER**, MORE ORDINARY **OCCASIONS** TOO.

ingredients

8 scoops of **vanilla ice cream**

5 measures/120ml/4fl oz/ ½ cup **advocaat**

2⅔ measures/60ml/4 tbsp freshly squeezed **lime juice**

freshly grated **nutmeg**

about 300ml/½ pint/1¼ cups chilled **lemonade**

1 Put half the vanilla ice cream in a food processor or blender and add the advocaat and the lime juice, with plenty of freshly grated nutmeg. Process the mixture briefly until well combined.

2 Scoop the remaining ice cream into four medium tumblers. Spoon over the advocaat mixture and top up the glasses with lemonade. Sprinkle with more nutmeg and serve immediately.

tip
Freshly grated nutmeg has a warm, nutty aroma and flavour that works as well in creamy drinks as it does in sweet and savoury dishes. A small nutmeg grater is a worthwhile investment if you don't have one.

strawberry daiquiri

method

BASED ON THE **CLASSIC** COCKTAIL, THIS VERSION IS A **WONDERFUL** DRINK WHICH RETAINS THE **ESSENTIAL** INGREDIENTS OF **RUM** AND LIME AND COMBINES THEM WITH **FRESH** STRAWBERRIES AND **STRAWBERRY ICE** CREAM TO CREATE A REFRESHING, THICK ICED **FRUIT** PURÉE.

ingredients

225g/8oz/2 cups **strawberries**, hulled

5ml/1 tsp **caster (superfine) sugar**

5 measures/120ml/4fl oz/½ cup **bacardi rum**

1⅓ measures/30ml/2 tbsp freshly squeezed **lime juice**

8 scoops of simple **strawberry ice cream**

about 150ml/¼ pint/½ cup chilled **lemonade**

extra **strawberries** and **lime** slices to decorate

1 Blend the strawberries with the sugar in a food processor or blender, then press the purée through a sieve into a bowl. Return the strawberry purée to the blender with the rum, lime juice and half the strawberry ice cream. Blend until smooth.

2 Scoop the remaining strawberry ice cream into four cocktail glasses or small tumblers and pour over the blended mixture.

3 Top up with lemonade, decorate with fresh strawberries and lime slices, and serve.

variation
Orange-flavoured liqueur or vodka could be used instead of the rum, if you prefer.

tip
For the best results use luxury, or preferably, homemade ice cream. This will avoid the risk of a synthetic flavour and garish colour.

ingredients

60ml/4 tbsp **drinking chocolate**

400ml/14fl oz/1⅔ cups chilled **milk**

150ml/¼ pint/⅔ cup **natural (plain) yogurt**

2.5ml/½ tsp **peppermint essence**

4 scoops **chocolate ice cream**

mint leaves, **chocolate shapes**, **chocolate curls** and **whipped cream**, to decorate

tip
Use cocoa powder instead of drinking chocolate if you prefer, but add sugar to taste.

iced mint & chocolate cooler

MANY **CHOCOLATE** DRINKS ARE **WARM** AND **COMFORTING**, BUT THIS ONE IS REALLY **COOL** AND **REFRESHING** – IDEAL FOR A **HOT SUMMER'S** DAY.

method

SERVES 4

1 Place the drinking chocolate in a small pan and stir in about 120ml/4fl oz/½ cup of the milk. Heat gently, stirring, until almost boiling, then remove from the heat.

2 Pour into a cold bowl or large jug and whisk in the remaining milk, yogurt and peppermint essence.

3 Pour the mixture into four tall glasses and top each with a scoop of ice cream. Decorate with mint leaves and chocolate shapes or whipped cream and chocolate curls. Serve them immediately.

coffee cognac cooler

THIS DRINK IS **UNABASHEDLY DECADENT** — NOT FOR THOSE **COUNTING** CALORIES!

method

SERVES 2

1 Shake or blend all the ingredients except the ice cream together.

2 Pour into tall glasses and gently add a scoop of ice cream to each. Decorate with chocolate shavings and serve with a long-handled spoon.

> **tip**
> The coffee liqueur can be either a cream-based one, such as Kahlúa, or a non-cream based liqueur, such as Tia Maria.

ingredients

250ml/8fl oz/1 cup cold strong darker-roast **coffee**

3½ measures/80ml/3fl oz/ 6 tbsp **cognac** or **brandy**

generous 2 measures/50ml/ 2fl oz/¼ cup **coffee liqueur**

50ml/2fl oz/¼ cup **double (heavy) cream**

10ml/2 tsp **sugar**

250ml/8fl oz/1 cup **crushed ice**

2 scoops **coffee ice cream**

chocolate shavings, to decorate

index